INVISIBLE EARTHQUAKE

A woman's journal through stillbirth

modjaji books

INVISIBLE EARTHQUAKE

A woman's journal through stillbirth

Malika Ndlovu

Publication © Modjaji Books 2009
Text © Malika Ndlovu 2009

First published in 2009 by Modjaji Books, CC
P O Box 385, Athlone, 7760
modjaji.books@gmail.com

ISBN 978-0-9802729-3-2

Book and cover design by Natascha Mostert
Edited by Colleen Crawford Cousins and Colleen Higgs
Cover Art by Colleen Crawford Cousins
Lettering by Hannah Morris
Photographer: Charley Pollard

Printed and bound by Megadigital, Cape Town
Set in Garamond 12/14 pt

For Iman Bongiwe Ndlovu

Born and buried
3rd January 2003

CONTENTS

2003

1st January, 15h05

I have just taken the tablet to catalyse the contractions that will deliver you, out of your nest, my womb. I sit with a lit candle in the garden, listening to a baby crying next door, wind blowing through the trees, a plane flying over high above. How do I leave home today full of you and come home tomorrow, empty? My mind swings between dead calm practicalities of to do lists and necessary arrangements, to tears cutting me down to a deep quiet grief I cannot fully feel even though I know it is there.

How could I imagine that your last fevered fluttering was goodbye? How can I hold the thought that you have been sleeping lifeless inside of me since then, already gone? It's been almost four days. I race from recollecting all the signs that came before to tell us that this was where your path would lead, signs that I shut out so many times, clear calls for me to face the silence of you no longer kicking within me.

This morning in the shower a clear image of these few words on a blank page came to me:

"Your death has changed my life."

11th January, 12h45

I am paralysed, yet I want to surrender. I'm surprised at how hours pass, days, now one week. I want to hold on, hold back, slow down for fear of further distance from you, from the sensitivity of my still-leaking breasts, from the flow of blood that still connects us so intimately. I don't want time to take these sensations of you away from me. I also want time to ease the sharp pain of memory that these bring so instantly.

Any moment could be the point of bursting, of breaking down at the sadness of our story, the cruel if-onlys and what-ifs. Baby items fall across my path unexpectedly and I must pack them away, not for two months till your due date, but for an indefinite period now.

I so much wanted to touch you. Now I nuzzle your brother a little deeper, a little longer than usual, imagining your satin-soft skin against my lips. I was afraid I might touch you too much, you – so fragile and pure, afraid too, of what holding you too long would do to me when the time for letting go came. So I tenderly stroked you with my fingertips and my breath. I wrapped you in a cloth that I knew I would bury too, my fiery yellow sarong. In the few hours we shared alone in that delivery room, I held you until my arms ached before putting you in the crib beside my bed, using a thin scarf to shade you from the glare of hospital lights and prying eyes of hospital staff checking in on me. I tried to maintain some kind of cocoon, the way mothers swaddle their newborns.

The days pass with or without my consent. I visit your grave
for the second time, on the seventh day since your birth
– one of the many, many cycles that call to be completed.
Since that turning point announcement of "no foetal
heartbeat" initiated me into that enormous clan who know
the death of a beloved.

I am shaped by your absence, haunted by the detail of you.

13th January, 00h40

No milk flowed today. The aches, the leaking and bleeding subside. I feel them fade like another sorrowful tide of goodbyes. Again I am letting go in ways I have no control over.

I chanted and sang with her on stage, played music with shakers and words. I soaked with her in bubble baths, smiled alone in the dark with my palms resting on either side of my naked belly, like two ever-eager ears straining for a hint to kick-start our midnight conversations. I felt her take over my body, creating that familiar feeling of unbalance as my back arched to compensate for a larger belly, forcing me into larger waistlines and super-comfy shoes, clicking my bones in and out of place, pinching a nerve here and there, making me jump or sit upright in pain or fright.

14th January, 22h02

What time zone is this? Fourteen days have escaped my grasp. The memory of you, the loss of you, separation from you is so present, yet I can also call it past. How can I lie in the same positions, wear the same shoes or preggy clothes, sit in the same chair, walk through the same house, when nothing is the same without you?

Everything has changed since you. I do not feel the same, breathe the same, think the same, see things in the same way. The only consistent element is your silence, your absence and the thin line of events that mark my mental calendar, the sudden fall from joyful anticipation to sorrow-filled waiting.

21st January, 12h05

I know you are no longer living
In my body
Everything repeats the same sad truth
That simple indigestible fact
Yet I am like a child shaking her head
In disbelief
It's only been two weeks
Almost three
Since you were here
Heart beating
Lungs breathing
Feet kicking, arms dancing
In me

I asked for aloneness, this retreat
To be closer to you
To recapture and try again
To come to terms
With what we've been through
Something so vital
Someone so precious
Has been severed from me
I cannot fathom how I am supposed to be
Separated from you physically
Wrap you up neatly in memory
Do anything with this hole in me
That only you could fill
I will never be walking
The way I used to walk this path
Now that I am walking without you

12th March, 09h35

Cigarettes put me in touch with my pain
Catch my breath
Coat my throat
I wrap my feet in new shoes,
My overweight body in new clothes
Dark and discreet.
Hair uncovered,
Toenails deep red,
Frida Kahlo feelings bleed
Into my heart and head.

16th March, 08h45

Blinded from my vision
Of a horizon
Including you
I feel my way into each day
I run
I hide
I collapse
I howl inside
My chest heaves
I smoke
Just barely keeping the breath flow
Oh, my baby, where did you go?

18th March, 19h37

Floating in and out of faith,
Disconnected,
I try to feel you, my baby,
But find myself absorbed instead
In my own sorrow at losing you
You tore my world in two
As earthquakes do.

20th March, 19h37

This is where the road separates
Those who have been there
And those who have not

Those who know
Drown in fresh air
In company
In shopping malls and parking lots
In circles of sympathizers
In the morning
At any given moment
In the middle of the night

Despite the love
Of those around me
I drown
In the silence
Rain cloud hanging heavy
Above the traffic of my thoughts
Around my still pounding heart
I drown
In the silence
Permeating my womb

23rd March, 10h25

I am so sore, but refusing to cry – again. I need solitude, but don't want to be alone. I am tired, but avoiding sleep. I do not want to run from thoughts of you or to escape this intense aliveness death has brought me.

9th April, 16h20

I light a candle for you, little-one-of-great-impact. You have reshaped me. Throughout my pregnancy you filled me with possibilities, a mother's blind projections. Now with equal force you have abruptly changed my direction. You are a fire burning strong and low. You have returned, only in spirit, to remind me that you did not come to bring me sorrow. Sorrow is not why you came.

17th April, 10h03

Of all the tormenting pictures in my head, the image of
your body, your blood draining from your limbs, your face,
collecting in your cavities, still brings me to my knees.
Blood, rose-red peeping from your lips, ears, nose, umbilical
cord, from between your legs. I am stained with this imprint
of your physicality. Blood curdling cries race through me, a
sound stream of desperation. I ache for a tangible trace of
you.

21st April, 20h03

Bongiwe, my beloved daughter,
My precious unseen one,
I take each step
In memory of you.
My body claims its breath
As yours no longer does.
My heart beats on
While yours is gone.

Bongi, my beloved one,
I am tossed,
I am torn,
I am stretched,
I am tested at each turn.
I keep moving, in honour of you.
I move because life and love surround me,
Urge me on.
Sometimes
I wonder
What you would wish
For me.

26th April, 10h26

Seven times in one day, seven conversations all about you, the all-round impact of you, my little Iman Bongiwe. Many times it was a comment about yearning to connect with you or asking where you are that started the tears. Yet now, a quiet morning after, I feel a release from the intensity of that wound. Me all around you, you all around me, in a way I have not recognized till now. I even project what " feeling connected" with you should be like. I imagine what sensations, what scenario will unfold. I don't know what form or sign I expect. What evidence am I waiting for that will bring the feeling of being consciously connected to you, my angel? I wait. I cry. I battle to digest the possibility that you never actually left me, that you are an enormous gift I simply struggle to receive. I ache to feel your presence, but then I reflect on each day and see that you have permeated every step.

28th April, 22h45

My lower back remembers. My breasts remember. My feet remember. When I see the thin film of sweat on my forearms, my eyes linger on the hair there. Your fragile forearms were covered with fine hairs too, an obvious beautiful affirmation that you came from me. The air I breathe thickens with memories.

1st May, 12h38

I'm navigating in and out
Of mental combat
Trying to figure
Exactly what station I've pulled into,
How to answer that simple question
How are you?

An invisible earthquake dulls my senses.
I hear myself speak
From a distance,
See their eyes blur in sympathy
Feel their embraces
Even in my suspension

From within the torn earth
Of my body
Which bears your death followed by your birth
Comes a gasp or a howl, or a laugh.
Sometimes I shrink into my jacket.
I wave goodbye and walk away.
There is nothing more to say.

3rd May, 00h05

Tonight I sit in the same Lazy-boy chair that I occupied so
often in those last weeks of pregnancy, facing in exactly
the same direction, pre-occupied with the same distraction
– TV. Hours pass as my chest quietly gets heavier and
heavier, till I have to switch the TV off. Silence settles in the
darkened room. Finally I allow the sadness to sink in.

27th May, 00h44

I write to keep you alive
I write to resist killing myself
In little do-able ways,
Lose days, dreaming of reunion with you.

I write to cleanse myself,
To release the river of sorrow
That circles and sometimes swallows me.

I write to remember the instants of acceptance,
A stream of light entering my imprisoned heart.
I write to liberate us both,
To continue our communication
Despite your eyes that never opened,
Your eyes that never met mine.

I write so that these words of love and yearning
Live longer than those that have fallen from my mouth,
Praying that you hear me now
Or maybe on some tomorrow
Out of my hands
Out of my time.

I write for women who know this
Unbearable
Unspeakable
Irreversible separation.
The desperation of clinging to sand
On that lonely shore
Where the ocean simply
Continues its rise and fall,

Persistently pushing and pulling us into a new day
Even when we thought we'd run out of ways
To live with this absence.

I write to relive the moments
That were only yours and mine,
To touch again
Your fragile skin,
Your delicate head,
To carefully lift your fingers one by one
Gently wrap them around my thumb.

I write to engrave you in memory,
To mark your place in our family.
I wake at dawn or wait for night
To have that sacred quiet
Where I can be alone with you,
Allowing the silence to open me up
And expose line by line
The feelings and thoughts
Caught in the safety-net
Of daytime composure.
At last I can drop the task
Of choosing when and when not
To mention your name
Of suppressing the impulse
To blurt it out to strangers.
Not lying or denying,
Simply not saying.

I write to run from forgetting,
To purge myself from the paralysis
Of knowing you are gone
Yet refusing to let go.
I write to calm my fear
Of losing all trace of you.
I write to draw myself out
Of the dark well of doubt.
I write to come to peace
With you being there
And my not yet knowing where

I write to keep myself
And you, my baby,
Alive.

22nd September, 18h28

I am lying in a doctor's examination room with my eyes
fixed on the ultrasound monitor. Where once I saw her
suspended in stillness, today I see the perfection of a son,
swimming within me. I feel a deep delight as I watch his
movements, hear his persistent heartbeat. Part of my heart
sinks silently too, now that it is clear no daughter will follow
her. She was the only one.

Almost seven days ago, a close friend died of cancer. Life
and death circle around me. I try to find my feet in each day,
knowing there are many ways to cry, that life goes on after
the body decays and that our spirits are what matters most,
while we live. I feel blessed and stretched anew.

3rd October, 10h30

In my backyard
Stands a gnarled old peach tree stump
Determinedly growing new branches,
Sprouting baby-pink flowers,
A shower of innocence
At Nature's command –
It's Spring!

Buttercup yellow sprays out
From the bush in the corner,
Between spiky green leaves
Baby's breath, white above the ferns
Sways in the wind
Down below the loquat tree
Almost at the centre of my garden
Miniature lilac daisies with yellow hearts
Blossom for Iman.

Where do I place my sadness?
What must I do?
Let it sit within me till it overflows from my eyes
unexpectedly?
Or let it come between an ordinary day and me?
What can I say that hasn't been said before?

2004

1st January, 22h35

It is irrevocably one year later and all that has happened
since then, the healing, the love, the pending birth of a third
son ... is all as it should be. All pull my focus back to life,
remind me of all my blessings, show me how the waves of
sorrow rise and fall with the passing of time and that I am
not in charge.

I have ached, I have sobbed, I have smoked, I have danced,
I have written, I have performed on stage. I have resisted,
I have surrendered, I have yearned, I have howled, I have
wondered, I have let go, I have questioned, I have relented
and all the while I have remembered and continue to
remember.

Yesterday I posed for a portrait of me in full-blown
motherhood again, my belly the centre of attention. While
my friend painted I heard myself say out loud, 'Each child
of mine has been a revolution.'

3rd January, 04h48

The wind wakes me for the third time, rattling the door
near my bed. Finally propelled out of bed I savour the early
morning sky, watch the garden being swept by the wind,
gently and vigorously in turn. I give praise for the *muthi* my
writing has been through every phase of this intense year.
Somehow I am here, one year later, one year older.

I resurrect the details of our separation, the sight of
you, finally free from my womb, the quiet of those few
subsequent hours alone with you, a part of me lying still
beneath the cloth I wrapped around you. Your smell, your
touch eludes me.

18th January, 20h56

Sadness descends
A gentle mantle
Inevitable as nightfall

No matter how full of light and distractions
This day has been
The emptiness of me without you
Seeps through
Stealing my words, my laughter
Drawing me back into quiet limbo
Where day after day I seem to go
For how long
I do not know

16th October, 21h45

A day of retreat. Distraction from the echo of a dream,
the second in a week about the death of my beloved.
Tears brim. Even the films I watch to avoid my thoughts
raise themes of grieving, a seemingly unbearable loss.
Menstruation finally comes. Irrational fears of pregnancy
disappear. A cleansing cycle begins. It is 21 months since my
angel flew away.

3rd November, 20h35

I cry at breakfast and on the phone to a friend, as we touch the almost two year old hole in my heart. Later I drive home, linger outside in my car, alone. My three sons are inside. I try to step outside my life.

I remember the moment when I finally said it out loud: I haven't felt any movement in the last few days. With those words a silent web began to spin itself around me, in between us, invisible and yet impossible to ignore. Events, incidents, moments, now begin to tie up, bringing my warning dreams into focus.

Somehow, suspended by shock and adrenalin, we went about the practical tasks of getting from point A to point B: digestible chunks of information. We waited for the final word from someone else, someone outside of ourselves and our subconscious knowing. There was no hurry. Time slowed down and our tolerance of this pace was not about patience but a growing icy paralysis, a gradual dawning of a giant chapter in our family history, in our relationship, in my life, in my body.

Each time I go within to remember, especially the fine details, each time I unwrap the tightly bound bandages around my chest, each time I go to that small patch of earth in an overgrown garden for the dead, something in me dies – and some part of me is more acutely alive. I walk away empty and full.

5th November, 14h18

I curled up into a ball, listening to the wind howl. I cried for her alone out there, with her tiny bones buried in the earth somewhere, so close yet so unreachable. The gusts of Nature's breath pull and tug at me, insisting that I let go, that I move on, telling me that my little girl did not come to weigh me down but to free me.

2005

3rd January, 12h03

I am in the back seat of the car, as we travel on a long hot
dusty Karoo road. For the last hour my thoughts have taken
me even further off. Laughter abruptly brings me back. My
sons jostle each other, their sticky hands and snack crumbs
all over me. The breeze through the window is warm,
bringing little relief from the heat. I ask if we can stop. For
a while my eye has been on the dashboard clock. Two years
ago, around this time, also on a Friday, we were burying her.

In the dust under a roadside tree I find exquisitely designed
seedpods. I take a few back home with me, to put on an
altar I have decided to make in memory of her. In some
ways I feel far from God, in other ways, closer than ever
before, all because of her.

16th February, 1645

Grief pulls your strings
After letting you loose long enough
So you will feel the weight of another fall

Grief calls you inside, locks you up
Takes you back
To childish threats and tantrums
None of which make any difference
To what happened, what can never be replaced

Grief knows your secret weaknesses
Your hiding places
Can turn the most ordinary places
Into alien landscapes

Grief changes your walk, your talk
Brings you unexpectedly to your knees
Grief ignores all your pleas

Grief makes you want to hurt yourself
Want to hold yourself back
When time pushes you forward

Grief tries to convince you
That nothing and no one can take its place
Grief pretends to disappear
Then jumps up in your face

Grief teaches you patience
Gives you no choice
Takes away your voice

Grief destroys all you have built
If you let it,
If you forget to give in

Grief is a cleansing fire; embrace it
Surrender to its demands
Grief knows the way

Within grief's cave
Under the spell of its darkness
The real healing work begins

8th November, 11h25

When her heart made music with mine
I was not listening
She told me she was saying goodbye
A simple parting sound
Then silence

In the days of knowing and not wanting to know
I watched my swollen belly grow soft with her leaving
When I could not hold on to anymore hours
I called for those who could help me let go
I wanted them to say with their equipment
What I knew but could not digest
I needed to see what only an ultrasound scan would show
But my first cry was No!

Soon I was under water
Mother Nature in charge
Coming up for air when she allowed me
Sinking back in
When the outside world began invading

Three years
Three sons
And still a womb full of tears
She left them there
Water for washing away my fears
I know she did not come to bring me sorrow

I have held on all this time
For another letting go
On this random day
Allowing everyone to know
That my heart still aches to the point of suffocation
To the point of lighting yet another bitter cigarette
Even to the point of wanting to sleep it all away

15th November, 10h22

This time
I am the crying newborn
Emerging from a womb of tears
My angel watches over me
Waiting patiently for me
To embrace her in delight
Only the ache of my human heart
Stands in the way

9th December, 15h55

When you finally
And suddenly
Left my womb
My trembling arms
My yearning gaze
I began unconsciously wrapping myself in a second skin
Spinning an invisible crystal thread around myself

I began to adapt to a new living
Slowing down my movement
My breathing
Wanting, some days, to die
Some nights, suspended in a pool of my own tears,
Affirming that I was still alive

Your dying changed every detail of my living
I could not recognize the eyes in my mirror
Feel the familiarity of my body as it once was
Only an aching awkwardness
An amputation that still had to register.
Even my skin felt too thin.
So began the spinning
Day after day into night into day
Circling myself in a ritual of sorrow
A concentrated circling of the wound
The deep tunnel it seemed you had slipped into
I was determined to follow
And find you

Sometimes my chest grew too heavy
I inhaled smoke instead of air
A secret torture
A silent ritual of remembrance
Expressing my burning
Holding myself in the moment
Not wanting time to move me forward
Or memory to take me back
Only the manageable size of each moment
Each breath was as far as I wanted to step

Soon almost a thousand days will have passed
My spinning long since come to an end
I have been in a cocoon of my own making
Playing alive
Playing dead
Even playing

Somewhere in this shadow pocket
I have reawakened
To my stillness
To my aloneness
A gentle recognition of my separateness
From all this weeping

I have found ways to allow and suppress my tears
Words to explain why I do
Perhaps only discovering parts of myself I never knew
Before you

As this third year closes I sense a fundamental shift
A crack in my shell
Where light has begun streaming in
Warming my new skin
In my heart I am standing on a cliff
Waiting for the wind to carry me
I will not leap or dive
I will not resist when that moment of flight arrives
In all this waiting and wishing
Raging and aching
Accepting and denying
I have developed a comfort in the dark
A hunger for the dawn
In my bones I know
I have grown wings

17th December, 20h17

A glacier in me has been breaking
Making immense
Yet silent
Slow
Shifts

I was initiated when Iman Bongiwe left
Now, almost three years later
A profound transition breaks
Much like dawn

I am surprised
By how much laughter can spill out of me
Even when I allow myself to dissolve into tears
I keep on shuttling the vast range of emotions
My spirit keeps moving
Even on days my body
Or my heart
Refuses to dance

22nd December, 08h35

A long road trip after a spontaneous visit to my hometown gives me space and time to read, write and ponder. This journey sets off a festive season of reunion with my extended family, my wide and entangled roots. There in the midst of loud chatter and music, the traffic of relatives of all ages, a newborn baby girl has landed, my aunt's third daughter, only three weeks old. Swaddled in pink she is still other-worldly, her random facial expressions, her faraway gaze, her fragile features and sudden reflexes all proof of her recent voyage from womb into the unfathomable space outside of that supreme haven.

My mother observes me, and her eyes well up with tears that in another moment, could easily be mine. " I know," I say to her in comfort and marvel at how my impulse has not been to make the connection between this little girl's presence in my arms and the absence of my own. Life is not static. I am alive.

A quiet new layer of acceptance has fallen into place that does not make me pain or pine as I embrace someone else's little girl. Those yearnings may return at any time, but this new station I have come to brings in the lightness of the moment where the past is not drawn into the present, has no relevance, except if I start embroidering that web. How easily it can be spun.

28th December, 18h00

In my heart's calendar I mark this day. The day my instincts told me three years ago that your heart had stopped beating, setting off three days of deep shock and protective denial, until I could not ignore your silence anymore. Your beautifully articulate almost-five-year-old brother has been talking about you more than usual lately. He tells everyone that he has — not had — a sister, but she died and, depending on his audience goes off into elaborate explanations of how you fell from the sky. His latest drawings of our family include you larger than anyone else.

"She is big and blue like the sky, so I made her big but this paper is not big enough," he confidently explains. He shares his dreaming of you and cannot describe a face or shape, just a certainty that it is you. I listen in quiet envy.

I have been afraid to call you back to me in this way. Afraid you will not come. Perhaps he is right. I could try his perspective. You are with us and have never left, endless and ever-present as the sky, holding us in a permanent embrace.

"I love you, Mummy and I am your alive son, my heart never stopped yet, hey?" Only I hear the relevance of his choice of words, the sore resonance of his question on this day, at this time.

2006

2nd January, 16h20

I visit your grave with seawater
Collected for cleansing,
Renewing my memories of you

Two sisters
My mother and aunt
Sing heartfelt hymns
Shed words and tears
Find their feet
And a renewed bond with each other
As we stand above your tombstone

What a miraculous way you have
Of grounding us in our truths
Your presence
Through memory or story
Reveals our interconnectedness
Your purpose
Is obvious
Simple
Divine

A sacred sharing
You at the centre
Allows me to walk away
Lighter

POST SCRIPT

January 2009

On the 3rd of January 2006 my mother, five close friends and I gathered on a beach at dawn and sat silently in the disappearing dark, listening to the sea. Witnessing the silhouetted mountain and horizon gradually birthed into the light, we finally broke the hush with a few soft, heart-spoken words. I gave each one a white daisy to cast into the waves and we each in our own time approached the icy water's edge and made our offerings to the sea and sky. Joy carried me at that moment, filled me with a deep gratitude for each precious one who supported me through my journey of recovery.

When I stepped into the water I walked till it washed up to my knees. As the sea swirled around me tugging at my feet in its retreat, I felt the same sudden powerlessness and aloneness of the moment of that single push that finally flushed her from my womb. I started to cry when an unexpected gust of wind caught my daisy, took it from my hand, helped me let it go. It floated away from me quietly. My heart, a fragile lotus, bravely peeled back another circle of petals. I felt myself open instead of close, felt the glow of her, my daughter, being proud of me. As the darkness faded my companions and I walked along the shore and collected smooth stones. I took some of these stones home to place on her spot in our garden under the loquat tree, where already a giant wishbone stands, a forked branch I found on another walk, on another day. Its still leans against that tree, not alive and green but bleached into a new beauty by the sun.

～

Recently I drove over a familiar railway bridge in a Cape Town suburb and as I got over the incline and approached the traffic light at a busy intersection ahead, I suddenly choked up at the sight of a building on the corner being torn down. A large metal ball pounded at its crumbling walls and several identical cranes circled like cold yellow vultures, waiting to collect the debris. This was not just any building. This was the hospital where my life as in an earthquake's aftermath, had split in two. Six years ago on New Year's Day I sat in my obstetrician's cubicle on the 4th floor of this hospital with my husband clasping one of my hands in both of his. Our eyes remained fixed on the small foetal monitoring screen while the doctor gently described the signs we should see and hear, to prove that our baby girl, after almost seven months in-utero, was no longer alive. Later that Wednesday evening we checked into a private room in the same building where eventually, after two surreal days and several attempts to induce labour, Iman Bongiwe was stillborn at 3:35am on Friday 3rd January 2003. That building has now been transformed into a corporate block with exclusive apartments in the top floor.

Joy Mc Pherson, the loving midwife who supported me throughout this and two other pregnancies, died of a brain tumour in 2007, after more than twenty years in midwifery. Except for the few birth photographs that Joy was wise and loving enough to take for me, the birth and death certificates we have locked in our safe, the small grave on a hill near our home, there is little physical evidence that our daughter ever existed. Yet, like that reconstructed building, the entire landscape of all our lives has fundamentally changed. Nothing can be as it was before. Time has relentlessly brought on this change and I am still taken by surprise some days, when I realise how much time has passed since that turning point, how I have ached and cried less and less, how I have found and developed ways to live with what I thought I couldn't and didn't want to bear in the beginning.

Just over a year after Iman Bongiwe's passing I gave birth to Kwezi Michio – who is now almost 5 years old. His was an unplanned-far-too-soon-but-then-again-perhaps-perfectly-timed pregnancy about which doctors and family alike held great fears and doubts. But he was born at home, he emerged safely from the very same womb in which she did not survive. His physical presence is for me inextricably connected to her physical absence. His growth and milestones hardly ever pass without my thoughts lingering, even for a second, on how it would be if she were here or remembering the depths of sorrow that he lifted me from when he entered our lives.

Still, with time and the many forms of healing I have chosen, the harsh strokes on this canvas of my heart have begun merging, blending, blurring so that I rarely think of what my eyes saw in those few hours of holding her tiny body or what I could still see in those few precious photographs. I don't choose to remember her that way. I am able to see her now, in my own way, everywhere and in everything. She is an inner compass for me, a reminder of what matters in this life, how fleeting it is, how fragile we are. She is fully present in our family memories, our occasional verbal recollections and in the lives of those who carried my family and I through the initial shock and heartbreak. For each of us in our individual experience of her, the cycles of grieving continue, and yet ebb with time. She lives through us and through all those whom her story, our story has made an impact on. Through this book that circle widens and the overwhelming silence and invisibility around her life and death and hopefully many others like hers, is penetrated.

ACCOMPANYING

Muriel Johnstone and Zubeida Bassadien, maternity hospital social workers, write about how they counsel women who have experienced stillbirth and neo-natal deaths of their babies and how they feel about these grieving women.

Muriel: *Nothing could have prepared me for the intense sadness I felt the first time I accompanied a mom to view her baby who had died a little earlier. If I was that overwhelmed by emotion, how must the mother feel who carried the infant for nine months and had bonded with the baby throughout her pregnancy?*

Walking through the passages of the Maternity hospital and hearing the jubilant sounds of mothers often makes me feel that pregnancy for most women is a happy, joyous event which brings with it a sense of great anticipation and expectation. The expectant mother looks forward to the birth of her baby. The birth signifies the start of a new life, which holds new meaning for the mother, the father and the rest of the family.

The death of the baby is a thought which probably seldom crosses the minds of parents, so when it occurs the intensity of the feelings of loss and sadness present a crisis which can be very difficult to deal with.

Muriel: *Having completed my family by the time I got to working at the Maternity Centre, I was not prepared for the feelings of thankfulness and appreciation I felt at having delivered three perfectly normal children. My pregnancies were difficult but at no stage did I think about losing a child. My initial experience of the death of an infant was shattering and forced me to look at childbirth in a very different light.*

Social workers within a maternity setting can offer an invaluable service in ensuring that every birthmother who experiences a stillbirth or neonatal death is provided with the opportunity to receive some kind of supportive counselling to enable them to begin to grieve.

Zubeida: *The connection made with a mother during counselling is often evident in the way she relates to me. It must be difficult to open up to someone you've just met. So it's important for me to make the mom feel that I really care and this should shine through in the way I conduct my work. My verbal and non-verbal communication should attest to the fact that I have her interests at heart.*

In counselling, we offer support to a mother who has experienced a loss. She will go through various stages in coming to terms with her loss. At first she is in shock, at having to deal with the death of her baby. This manifests itself in different ways. Some women are completely numbed by the experience whilst others express their feelings in tearfulness, emotional outbursts or unusual behaviour.

As counsellors we are aware of the feelings and behaviours experienced after death and our comfort, support and ability to provide a safe environment for the expression of these feelings can help to alleviate some of the distress felt by the birthmother.

Zubeida: *This is a rewarding experience for me as a social worker as the one-to-one time spent with a grieving mother is mutually beneficial to both of us. It allows for personal introspection and has indeed given me a new perspective on life and the inevitability of death.*

Denial is common at this stage even if the mother has taken the opportunity to view and hold her baby. Mothers often start believing that baby is only asleep and will wake up at a later stage. In these cases no amount of convincing the mother otherwise will change her belief and staff are encouraged to allow this phase of grieving to be and just provide supportive care. Denial, as with many other reactions to death, is a human way of coping with and defending against something so painful and distressing that it feels unbearable.

For all women, the loss of their baby is a very individual, personal experience. Many birthmothers, especially in public hospitals, face the birth of a stillborn on their own and feel an overwhelming sense of guilt and self-blame at the loss of the child. Birthmothers tend to experience enormous feelings of failure and inadequacy at the inability to bring a child or grandchild into the family.

Often, the mother's guilt and self-blame are further exacerbated by the lack of an explanation as to how the death occurred. This can result in the mother resorting to a great deal of self-exploration and self-reflection. Questions arise as to why and how the death occurred and what could have prevented the loss. When no explanation is forthcoming, the mother rationalises and sometimes immerses herself in self-blame and guilt.

Zubeida: *Perhaps this is the most difficult part of helping a mother come to terms with her loss. How do I convince a mom that she is not responsible for her baby's death? For her this is real and she seems to feel that she has to have answers to all the questions mulling around in her mind.*

Anger often surfaces in counselling sessions. Mothers and even family members express anger at all those who are around. Doctors, nurses and other staff are sometimes blamed for not having done enough to prevent the death of the infant. As counsellors we are aware that anger is real and it is also displaced as it is sometimes used as a coping mechanism to mask the extreme pain felt at the loss. Our task is to allow mothers and families to ventilate these feelings. Our acknowledgement and validation of their feelings sometimes serves as a temporary measure in easing the pain they are experiencing at this time. We realise that confronting the anger at this stage may not help, but mothers and families are encouraged to put pen to paper in helping to dispel the anger felt immediately after birth.

No counselling session is complete without the mother being offered the opportunity to view her baby. Photographs, footprints and other mementoes of the baby are also tangible reminders of the baby which may help relieve the pain of grieving in the long term.

Zubeida: *I have to keep reminding myself that the anger is not directed at me.*

For those mothers leaving the facility, the danger always exists that the already difficult grieving process can go awry.

At home, mothers usually have an innate need to appear strong, so they have difficulty in expressing their feelings.

Families, too, do not understand the enormity of the loss and inadvertently resort to clichés which encourage the mother to get on with her life.

Many people believe that the mother never really knew her baby and therefore she should not experience these intense emotions.

Muriel: *I can imagine the sadness at having to leave hospital without a baby in your arms. What does one say to the children at home and to others who come around to see the newborn infant? Have I prepared the mother enough to deal with these situations?*

Our role prior to discharge is to make the mother and family aware of the need to grieve. The mother needs to feel justified in her grief and should be allowed to feel the sadness and the pain she is feeling. Grieving is a process and therefore healing only occurs with time.

Each mother grieves in her own way. Each experiences a unique sense of loss, which is manifested in different ways and needs to be dealt with accordingly.

What we do however believe is that our treatment of the mother in the hospital, her encounter with various professionals and the understanding and support she receives all help to facilitate her recovery after such a distressing experience.

Muriel: *My counselling has to be worthwhile. If not, what is the point? I have an innate desire to always feel with and for my patients, so it's not unusual to shed a tear at times. Each patient, to me, is unique in her grief and so I try to treat each one as a unique being.*

WOMEN AND STILLBIRTH:
a medical perspective
by Sue Fawcus

I am a specialist obstetrician working at a large public sector maternity hospital in South Africa, serving women from disadvantaged communities in and around Cape town.

My job involves great extremes: quietly observing the powerful natural birth process but aggressively intervening at the sudden onset of a life-threatening emergency; acknowledging the wonderful joy of the newborn as well as sharing and managing the devastating pain of the women whose babies are stillborn or die soon after birth.

What is a stillbirth?

A stillborn baby (stillbirth) is one that is born with no sign of life. Such babies have died in the womb before birth. If the fetus (as we call babies in the womb) never develops, or dies in the first five months of pregnancy, this sad event is known as a miscarriage, since at this early stage, the fetus is not sufficiently developed to survive outside the womb. A fetus that dies later in the pregnancy (from six months to nine months) was potentially capable of life outside of the womb. It dies inside the womb (intrauterine death) and is born as a stillbirth. Sometimes the baby has been dead in the womb for several days or weeks before birth; in other circumstances the baby dies during the process of labour.

We who work in maternity hospitals know the extent of the problem of stillbirths, but it is not generally known in the community at large, and for the individual pregnant woman who has never ever contemplated such a possibility, the information that her baby has died in her womb is catastrophic news.

How common is stillbirth?

In South Africa in 2006 there were approximately 19,500 stillbirths.[1] There are roughly 24 stillborn babies for every thousand births (2.4%).[2] This means that a busy maternity hospital that delivers over 600 babies per month would see more than three stillborn babies per week. Countries with much higher stillbirth rates include Nepal (55 per 1000 births or 5.5%) and Malawi (39 per 1000 births or 3.9%).

Well-resourced countries such as the UK and the Scandinavian countries have much lower stillbirth rates, approximately 4.4 per 1000 births (or 0.4%).

Who is at risk?

Stillbirths are more common in women younger than 18 years old and older than 35, in women with medical problems such as diabetes and HIV, and in women who smoke cigarettes or drink excessive amounts of alcohol during pregnancy. They are more common in poor women, who in addition may face obstacles accessing health care. However, many women without any of these risk factors also experience stillbirth.

What causes stillbirth?

In South Africa, the Perinatal Problem Identification Programme (PPIP) has been collecting data on stillbirths and newborn deaths since 1999. Data collected from 164 maternity sites (2003-2005) in South Africa were collated into a report, "Saving Babies", published in 2007.[2] The causes of 9 943 stillbirths were investigated. The report showed many causes for stillbirths. A tiny percentage (1.6% and 2.9% respectively) was because the mother had a pre-existing illness or the fetus failed to grow in the womb (intra uterine growth restriction). Three percent of the stillbirths occurred because the fetus was abnormal in some way. Infection during pregnancy or labour caused 5.1% of the stillbirths. Premature birth accounted for 10.4% of the stillbirths – the mother had gone into labour much too early, well before nine months; and 11.2% of stillbirths occurred because the baby became short of oxygen during the labour itself (intrapartum hypoxia). Thirteen percent of the stillbirths that occurred because the mother had bled from her womb in late pregnancy (placental abruption). Pre-eclampsia, a condition that causes dangerously raised blood pressure in pregnancy, caused 14.1% of the stillbirths.

What is worrying is that in 37.7%, or more than twice the number of the highest known cause of stillbirth (pre-eclampsia), no cause could be found. In some cases this may reflect that there were limitations on the resources needed to investigate every stillbirth adequately, but it also points to gaps in medical knowledge. We do not know why some stillbirths occur.

It is very difficult for a woman when there is no known reason for her baby's stillbirth. In these circumstances a woman may develop her own, faith-based explanation. Often women tend to blame themselves and may carry a lot of guilt for the stillbirth, which must double the pain experienced.

Can stillbirths be prevented?
Many (but not all) stillbirths can be prevented.
For example, a screening test for syphilis performed at the first antenatal visit will identify infected women who need treatment. This treatment can prevent the death of a baby from congenital syphilis.

Monitoring the mother's progress and the baby's heartbeat in labour, and performing an emergency caesarean section when problems arise can, in some circumstances, prevent the baby dying from lack of oxygen during labour (intrapartum hypoxia).

However, some problems occur so suddenly that despite the mother seeking medical help immediately, the baby is already dead in the womb. An example of this is a condition that causes the placenta (afterbirth) to separate from the wall of the womb and bleed (placental abruption). This can occur without any warning and results in the sudden death of the fetus.

The high number of stillbirths in South Africa would be reduced by poverty alleviation and community development, education about smoking and drinking in pregnancy, greater access to antenatal care, and greater access to adequately staffed preventive and emergency maternity services.

What is the risk of having a second stillbirth?
Women who have experienced a stillbirth are terrified of having another, some to the extent of avoiding ever having another pregnancy. Although some causes of stillbirth – such as when the placenta separates suddenly from the wall of the womb – may recur, others are unlikely to recur (such as syphilis, or hypoxia – the death of the baby during childbirth through lack of oxygen) and can be more easily prevented in another pregnancy.

What are the effects of having a stillborn baby for the mother?
This can only really be expressed by the women themselves, and is reflected in the moving testimony that forms the core of this book. I can only report what I have observed during my 30 years of working as the doctor involved when a woman

receives the shocking news that her baby has died inside her womb.

The mother often suspects a problem because she may not have felt the baby kick for a few days. At the clinic I try to find the baby's heartbeat with my stethoscope, sensing the anxiety in her eyes and voice. I then suggest an ultrasound, still keeping alive the possibility that perhaps I just could not hear the baby's heart beat.

The ultrasound gives the final answer. The baby's heart is not beating. I then break the news to the mother, always wondering what words to use. "Your baby is dead", feels very harsh.

The mother's initial response is shock and disbelief. She seems to enter a zone where there is no future and no ground from which to make the next move. A death always has its tragedy and sorrow, but when the dead being is inside one's own body the sorrow has an added dimension. Next, she shares this news with her partner and her family. I sense that the mother often carries a deep sense of guilt and inadequacy, which is undeserved, and about which I try to reassure her.

Plans have to be made: does she go home for a few days to be with her family, but what if people who don't know what has happened ask her about her baby? Does she stay in hospital and does she want us to induce her labour? The most common instinctive response seems to be for her to choose to have her labour induced, and to deliver her stillborn infant before she goes home.

Labour is a painful process, usually endured and survived because of the knowledge of the coming of the new life.

When endured without this endpoint, the physical pain of the contractions must compound the emotional pain and feeling of "deadness" inside. This may be made worse if a woman is alone in her labour, yet surrounded by many other women in other cubicles in the labour ward, and the sounds of the first cries of their live babies.

When the baby is born, most women want to see their baby, establish its gender and hold the baby. And there is much evidence to suggest that seeing or holding the baby helps the grieving process. Some mothers may be scared to see and hold their baby especially if it is abnormal or has been dead for many days, in which case it may look disfigured. Some sit quietly holding their stillborn baby for as long as they can stay in the labour ward. Small mementos such as a lock of hair, footprints, or sometimes a photograph can provide comfort as memory of this life-altering event.

The loss of her baby must feel cruelly emphasised by the surrounding mothers with live babies, and her engorged leaking breasts can only serve as a painful reminder of the life that could not be.

Grieving for a stillborn baby is a very lonely experience. The bereaved mother is the only one who ever really knew and experienced the baby. For others in her social and working circle it may seem like the loss of something that "never was". To the woman the loss is very real. Apart perhaps from a close partner, no one else can reminisce with memories of the baby. Going home means trying to start again, not pregnant and without the expected baby. Facing family and other children and dealing with their disappointment, as well, is even more difficult. What answers can she give to all those questions?

Typically, grief passes through all the stages of shock, denial, anger (questioning: "if only" "what if"), depression, and finally acceptance.

Health workers often recommend, for both physical and emotional reasons, that the woman waits at least one year before starting another pregnancy. At the time of delivery, talking of "next time" is premature. From reading Malika's story I have learned that there may be acceptance and there may be other successful pregnancies, but the sorrow and her stillborn child is never forgotten.

What is our role as health workers?
We can be advocates for improved perinatal care. We can be informed by national audits, such as PPIP, which reveal the causes of stillbirths and potential remediable factors, so that we can translate appropriate recommendations into policies and actions.

At the hospital level, staff may also feel traumatised by the delivery of a stillborn infant. Young medical or midwifery students may struggle to deal with their own feelings while supporting a woman who delivers a stillborn baby. However most hospitals have a system of review and discussion of every baby who dies. This may take the form of a weekly or monthly meeting attended by doctors and midwives where they discuss the cause of the death and whether it could have been prevented. Recommendations are made about the care of the mother in her next pregnancy, and plans are made to implement immediate changes to prevent (if possible) deaths of a similar nature.

At the personal level, doctors like myself need to "break the news" and offer immediate comfort to the mother.

Sometimes other emergencies mean that the doctor isn't able to spend sufficient time with the mother after breaking the news. Social workers and/or other health professionals skilled in bereavement counseling provide an invaluable role in supportive counseling at the time of the initial news, after delivery, and before going home.

I feel my role is to care, to be gentle, not to engender guilt, and to help the mother feel secure and contained. Staff who feel awkward in dealing with a grieving mother and avoid her could make her feel even more "abnormal".

It is always difficult to choose the right words, but 'being there', continuing to engage and providing kindness goes a long way. Occasionally the sorrow of the situation influences me and I wonder how the tears in my eyes that don't fall make her feel. Am I acknowledging her grief enough, or too much?

It is important for the health worker to be very attentive during the induced labour of a woman who is experiencing stillbirth. The fact that there is no need to monitor the baby's heart beat could mean she has less attention from the staff than other women in labour, which may only serve to emphasise her "differentness". In a busy maternity unit, after she has delivered the mother will go to a ward with other mothers and their newborn babies. I have found the other mothers are usually very caring in this difficult situation, and contrary to what I used to think, it may be better for her to be with others than being in a room on her own.

In the initial phases, the woman needs information about what is to happen about induction and the delivery, breast care after delivery, and so on, but she is still in shock. She is not ready to engage in a detailed discussion. It is better to wait until about six weeks later when the results of tests on the placenta and her blood, or a postmortem, has provided us with the cause of her baby's death.

At this visit it is more possible to have a "rational" discussion about what happened and why her baby died. Unfortunately, grief may also be rekindled by returning to the place where the baby died, and by seeing other pregnant women. Nevertheless, a good discussion and explanation can be facilitated. This is the time to discuss future pregnancies and what could happen differently. Some preventive measures may be under her control, for example, stopping smoking. Other advice might relate to early screening and intervention by a health worker. I usually provide the mothers with a letter summarising what happened, with specific recommendations for her next pregnancy. She can present this during her next pregnancy whenever she attends the clinic for check-ups.

Some women are still very traumatised at the six-week stage and may benefit from further professional counseling.

I frequently care for women who have had a stillbirth in their preceding pregnancy. The anxiety of the woman during her pregnancy and labour, and that of the attending staff, is palpable. It is very touching to see her this time around, holding a live baby in her arms. However I know, as Malika's story confirms, that a new birth cannot cancel out the previous death of a baby. It cannot replace the loss, but it can serve to provide a new source of great joy.

I have learnt a lot from reading Malika's story and I hope these comments help to provide further understanding to women who have suffered a stillbirth.

REFERENCES

1. Lawn JE, Kerber K, eds. *Opportunities for Africa's Newborns: practical data, policy and programmatic support for newborn care in Africa.* Cape Town; PMNCH, Save the Children, UNFPA,UNICEF,USAID,WHO;2006
2. Pattinson RC ed. *Saving Babies 2003-2005: Fifth perinatal care survey of South Africa.* Pretoria, MRC, CDC: 2007

References

RESOURCE LIST

Books

Ash, L *Life Touches Life: A Mother's Story of Stillbirth and Healing* (2004) NewSage Press

Davis, D *Empty Cradle, Broken Heart: Surviving the Death of Your Baby* (Revised) 1996 Fulcrum Publishing

Don, A *Fathers Feel Too* (2005) Bosun Publications

Douglas, A & Sussman, J *Trying Again: A Guide to Pregnancy After Miscarriage, Stillbirth and Infant Loss* (2000) Taylor Trade Publishing

Gamino, L *When Your Baby Dies through Miscarriage or Stillbirth* (2002) Augsburg Fortess Publishers

Henley, A & Kohner, N *When a Baby Dies: The Experience of Late Miscarriage, Stillbirth and Neonatal Death* (Revised) (2001) Routledge

Isle, S *Empty Arms: Coping After Miscarriage, Stillbirth and Infant Death* (Revised) (2000) Wintergreen Press

Kohn, I, Moffitt, P & Wilkins, I *A Silent Sorrow: Pregnancy Loss – Guidance and Support for You and Your Family* (2nd Edition) (2000) Brunner-Routledge

Nelson, T *A Guide for Fathers: When a Baby Dies* (Revised) (2007) Tim Nelson

O'Keeffe Lafser, C *An Empty Cradle, a Full Heart: Reflections for Mothers and Fathers After Miscarriage, Stillbirth or Infant Death* (1998) Loyola Press

Rank, M *Free to Grieve: Healing and Encouragement for Those Who Have Suffered Miscarriage and Stillbirth* (2004) Bethany House

Schott, J, Henley, A & Kohner, N *Pregnancy Loss and the Death of a Baby: Guidelines for Professionals* (2007) SANDS

Seftel, L *Grief Unseen: Healing Pregnancy Loss Through the Arts* (2006) Jessica Kingsley Publishers

Vredevelt, P *Empty Arms; Hope and Support for Those Who Have Suffered a Miscarriage, Stillbirth or Tubal Pregnancy* (2001) Multnomah Books

Wood, S & Fox, P *Dying: A practical guide for the Journey* (2005) Double Storey Juta

Wunnenberg, K *Grieving the Child I Never Knew* (2001) Zondervan

Books For Children

Brown, L & Brown, M *When Dinosaurs Die: a Guide to Understanding Death*, Little, Brown and Company

Goldman, L *Children Also Grieve, Talking About Death and Healing*, Jessica Kingsley Publishers

Rosen, M *Michael Rosen's Sad Book*, Walker Books Ltd

Savage, J *Toby's Tiny Tot* (2006) Bosun Publications

Schwiebert, P *We Were Gonna Have a Baby, But We Had an Angel Instead* (2003) Grief Watch

Sunderland, M *Helping Children with Loss: A Guidebook*, Speechmark

WEBSITES

International Stillbirth Alliance
A non-profit coalition of organizations dedicated to understanding the causes and prevention of stillbirth.
www.stillbirthalliance.org

Empty Cradles
An online memorial for babies lost to miscarriage, stillbirth, infant loss or SIDS.
www.empty-cradles.com

SANDS: Stillbirth and Neonatal Death Society
A UK charity providing support for bereaved parents and their families. Books and other publications can be ordered from their website.
www.uk-sands.org

The Compassionate Friends
http://www.tcfcape.co.za/stillbirth.htm

Khululeka – To Be Free
Grief and Loss Support for Children and Youth
www.khululeka.org

SUPPORT GROUPS AND ORGANISATIONS IN SOUTH AFRICA

Bereavement Support Group for Stillbirth and Neo-natal Death
To meet other parents who have suffered stillbirth or neo-natal death or to start a support group, contact Nicole or Graeme at: bornsleeping@gmail.com

The Compassionate Friends
Telephone numbers:
- 086 122 7464 (Monday to Friday 11am to 3pm)
- 011 - 4406322
- 013 - 7524450
- 021 - 4389357

E-mail: support@tcfcape.co.za

Lifeline
24 hour crisis telephone number: 086 132 2322
National office toll free number: 0800 012 322

Peter Fox, Bereavement Counsellor & Spiritual Director at St. Lukes Hospice (CT)
- 021 - 797 5333

Cell: 083 293 4630

ACKNOWLEDGEMENTS

I offer sincere gratitude to the medical and alternative healers who helped me to deliver my baby girl and ground myself in the critical weeks that followed. These include my one-of-a-kind midwife the late Joy Mc Pherson of Midwives Inc., Specialist Obstetrician Dr. Razak Dhansay, Dr. Laszlo D. Zsory - Obstetrician and Life Energy Therapist, Clinical Psychologist Ruth Ancer and in later months Kim Palmer of Compassionate friends, alternative healers Rob Harrington, Gillian Barton, Dr. Victor Luies and Dr S V Bulatov homeopath, iridologist and nutritionist and Dr. Carol Thomas - Specialist Obstetrician and gynaecologist.

To the extended sisterhood I am privileged to share my life with: Deirdre Rhodes, Iman Rappetti, Stacey Munsamy, Zulfah Otto-Sallies, Carla Rafinetti, Bettina Schouw, Ernestine Deane, Rudayba Petersen, Kyoko Kimura, Pregs Govender, Nomfundo Walaza, Ingrid Askew, Khadija Heeger, Gabrielle le Roux, Shira Jankelson-Groll, Eugenia "Jenny" Canau & the Mama Tribe, Nancy Richards, Lorelle Royeppen-Viegi, Chantal Snyman, Carmen Myles, Debbie Mari, Penny Gaines, Mavis Smallberg, the late Zurayah Abass, Fatima Dike, Anne Schuster, Sue Bailey, Gabeba Baderoon, Lucille Lückhoff and numerous loving friends who supported me in the first critical months of coming to terms with this body and soul shock, continuing to carry me.

Deep thanks to Catharina Belgraver, Annie Dower who shared their stillbirth experiences and journeying through grief, even though we'd never met face to face. And all who have walked this path with me to date, there are too many to mention.

To my close friends and wonderful fellow artists who "lived with" my initial manuscript for a while, then offered their gifts of visual images in response: Gabrielle Le Roux, Kadiatou Diallo, Daya Heller, Garth Erasmus and the late Lallie Wagner.

To distinguished editors Shauna Wescott and Colleen Crawford-Cousins, as well as the many friends and fellow writers who gave me constructive feedback and their encouragement towards the birthing of this book.

To Colleen Higgs of Modjaji Books for giving my offering a home under her wide and nurturing branches by choosing to publish this book.

Sincere thanks to Sue Fawcus, Zubeida Bassadien and Muriel Johnstone of Mowbray Maternity Hospital who have generously shared the wisdom of their personal experiences, endorsing the relevance of this book in their work with mothers and in the world at large.

Finally to my incredibly loving and supportive family, without whom I could not have found ways daily, to keep moving through this profound experience of loss and living, particularly my parents Cecelia Dunn and Michael Conning, my husband Sensei Thulani Ndlovu, my wise and beautiful sons Rayne, Kamal and Kwezi - whose mere existence heals, anchors and inspires me.

AUTHOR'S BIO

Durban born writer Malika Ndlovu is the author of three books of poems, Born in Africa But, Womb to World: A Labour of Love and Truth is both Spirit and Flesh. She is a well-known poet, performer, and playwright whose published works have been performed on both local and international stages. Malika is a founder-member of the women writers' collective WEAVE, and co-editor of Ink @ Boiling Point: A selection of 21st Century Black Women's writing from the Southern Tip of Africa. She is the curator of the Africa Centre's poetry project Badilisha! – An African Poetry Exchange.

Her numerous performances, collaborations and festival appearances include: Poetry Africa; And The Word Was Woman Ensemble; Cape WOW (Women of the World) Festival; The Cape Town Festival; Mother City Book Festival; Mothertongue; Womantide; Wordwise: A Celebration of World Poetry Day.

She lives in Cape Town with her husband and three sons.